Who Is Jesus?

Scripture text from
The Contemporary English Version

• *The Baptism of Jesus*   2

• *The Temptations of Jesus*   8

• *The Prayer of Jesus*   14

• *Who Is Jesus?*   20

• *The Transfiguration*   26

• *The Main Events of Jesus' Life*   32

AMERICAN
BIBLE
SOCIETY

The Baptism of Jesus

Artists often use details like clues to help people to enter into a painting and enjoy it. How does this artist show that this is a very special moment in Jesus' life?

Paolo Caliari
Known as **Veronese**,
(1528-1588),
"The Baptism of Jesus"

© Alinari - Giraudon / Pitti Palace, Florence (Italy)

In Jesus' Day

The Story of Qumran

In Jesus' day, life was not always easy. There were many poor people. There were farmers without land, workers without jobs, and sick people who were not being looked after. There were also those who looked after themselves without giving the slightest thought to others. John,* the son of a priest from Jerusalem, realized that things had to change. He went off to the desert** where he led a very simple life. Yet large crowds followed him to listen to what he preached. He called for a change of heart, for conversion from one way of living to another. He spoke in the name of God, like the prophets of earlier times.

John invited his listeners to be plunged into the waters of the River Jordan in order to be baptized. They would come out clean in more ways than one. Being clean on the outside was the sign that their hearts had changed. Jesus and John belonged to the same family. In fact, they were cousins. Around A.D. 30, Jesus heard what people were saying about John, and so Jesus left Nazareth*** to visit his cousin John. He asked John to baptize him. John saw that his cousin was an extraordinary man, but at that time he still did not fully understand who Jesus was.

* John
John, the son of Zechariah, became known as John the Baptist because he baptized people in the Jordan River after they had turned back to God.

** Desert
In the Judean Desert, not far from Jerusalem, was a community of Jewish believers at a place called Qumran. In 1947 the "Dead Sea Scrolls," part of this community's library, were discovered. It is possible that John had some dealings with these people.

*** Nazareth
This is the village where Jesus spent most of his life. He worked with his hands, making things from wood (as a carpenter or joiner) and metal.

When Mark Wrote

Mark most likely wrote his Gospel around A.D. 70, some forty years after he had met Jesus. Mark wanted to proclaim the good news and to show that Jesus' baptism was just the start of a marvelous story. That's why he uses very striking and powerful imagery to describe it. The Spirit comes down like a dove. God's voice announces to everyone that Jesus is his own dear Son. Jesus' baptism marks the beginning of his ministry.

Nazareth today

On the Banks of the Jordan

Mark 1.4-11

So John the Baptist showed up in the desert and told everyone, "Turn back to God and be baptized! Then your sins will be forgiven."

From all Judea and Jerusalem crowds of people went to John. They told how sorry they were for their sins, and he baptized them in the Jordan River.

John wore clothes made of camel's hair. He had a leather strap around his waist and ate grasshoppers and wild honey.

John also told the people, "Someone more powerful is going to come. And I am not good enough even to stoop down and untie his sandals. I baptize you with water, but he will baptize you with the Holy Spirit!"

About that time Jesus came from Nazareth in Galilee, and John baptized him in the Jordan River. As soon as Jesus came out of the water, he saw the sky open and the Holy Spirit coming down to him like a dove. A voice from heaven said, "You are my own dear Son, and I am pleased with you."

Baptized with the Spirit

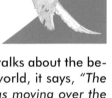

To be baptized with the Spirit means to be filled with the Holy Spirit. The first Christians considered the coming of the Spirit at Pentecost as a baptism in the Spirit.

Like a Dove

When the Bible talks about the beginning of the world, it says, *"The Spirit of God was moving over the waters."* The image is like a mother bird that hovers over her nest. When Mark talks about the beginning of Jesus' work, he says that the Spirit came down on Jesus *"like a dove."*

My Beloved Son

The first Christians, for whom Mark was writing, believed that Jesus was the true and beloved Son of God.

Beloved of God

Present Times

Today war shows its ugly face in many countries. Racism leads to hatred, which then sometimes leads to violence. Some people collapse under the weight of riches and too many possessions, while others die from hunger and poverty. Peace is blocked by people who stubbornly refuse to talk to or respect one another. Evil too often finds a home in our world.

Change

Wickedness, jealousy, revenge, envy, and evil desires spring up in the human heart and take root. So, if we want to change the world, we first have to change our hearts. From within our hearts we have to turn away from the dark power of evil and turn (be converted) toward the light of God.

A Sign

Jesus did not need to have a conversion of heart. There was no evil in him! When Jesus accepted John's baptism, it was a sign. Jesus is declaring war on the evil that can control and damage human beings. Jesus calls on all who believe in him to begin with a change of heart and turn away from the world of evil.

Beloved Children

Jesus is God's beloved Son. He became one of us and lived among us. He reveals (makes known) to us God's unending and limitless love. He tells us how to conquer the evil that lurks in our hearts and in the world: to behave as God's beloved children. This means loving God and our neighbor with all our heart and soul.

Mission

Christians have been given the job of fighting evil at the front line. Those who bear the name of Christ, God's beloved Son, have a critical mission. They must show by their words and deeds that true happiness will come only if people behave like children of God and do all they can to love their brothers and sisters everywhere.

Baptized

They are baptized.
Water poured in God's
own name:
Father, Son and Holy Spirit.
Sign of new life, freely given,
Opening up for everyone.
All, by God, called to be
One family.

"God's Beloved": will they live faithful to
this lovely name?

Baptized now, the love of Christ
In each heart is planted deep.
All to him, and each to all
Sisters now and brothers.
Called to live his gospel way
Day by day.

"Christ's One Body": will they love God
and neighbor like their Lord?

Baptized now, the Spirit's power
Through them flows to every place;
Strength to build a world that's new
Offering hope for everyone.
In the Spirit called to be
Strong and free.

"Spirit-filled": will they go
to spread God's word?

The Temptations of Jesus

The medieval artist has painted the power of evil as a half-human, half-devil figure. He shows Jesus being tempted three times. Read the account in Mark's Gospel to learn about these three temptations.

"The Mirror of Human Salvation"
"The Temptation of Christ"
(Mss. 139/1363 fol.14 V), fifteenth century

© Lauros-Giraudon / Condé Museum, Chantilly (France)

Jesus Was Tempted

Judean Desert

Just like us, Jesus had to choose between good and evil. Like us he had to choose between right and wrong, forgiveness or revenge, forgetting about himself and thinking of others instead.

After his baptism by John and before he began his public ministry, Jesus went off into the desert. His friends saw him leave, and they saw him come back. Although none of them saw what happened in the desert, they gradually understood that it was in the desert that Jesus chose the path he was going to follow: "To serve and not to be served."

*From Thailand,
a carved image of a demon*

The Temptations as Seen in the Gospels

Many years later, the Gospel writers Matthew, Mark and Luke told the story of Jesus. They put the account of the temptations in the desert at the start of their Gospels. They talk about this event as forty* days of thinking, being alone, and fasting. The temptation of Jesus is portrayed as a struggle between two spirits: the Spirit** of God and the spirit of evil, which they call the Devil.***

In their stories, these Gospel writers describe three temptations that Jesus avoided – the temptation to take the easy way out (changing stones into bread); the temptation to show off (jumping off the top of the Temple); and the temptation to claim power (taking God's place). As Christians we also are tempted with such desires. Though Jesus was tempted as we are, he came out the winner in his fight against the spirit of evil.

* Forty
In the Bible, the number forty is sometimes not to be taken as an exact figure. It is often used symbolically to indicate that this is a holy period of time, a period of reflection and of traveling toward God.

** Spirit
According to the Gospels, it's the Spirit of God that leads Jesus out into the desert.

*** Devil
This word comes from the Greek word "diabolos" and means "someone who speaks evil." In the Gospels, "the Devil" is considered the chief demon or chief evil spirit.

9

In the Desert

Matthew 4.1-11

The Holy Spirit led Jesus into the desert, so that the devil could test him. After Jesus had gone without eating for forty days and nights, he was very hungry. Then the devil came to him and said, "If you are God's Son, tell these stones to turn into bread."

Jesus answered, "The Scriptures say:

'No one can live only on food.

People need every word that God has spoken.'"

Next, the devil took Jesus to the holy city and had him stand on the highest part of the temple. The devil said, "If you are God's Son, jump off. The Scriptures say:

'God will give his angels orders about you.

They will catch you in their arms,

and you won't hurt your feet on the stones.'"

Jesus answered, "The Scriptures also say, 'Don't try to test the Lord your God!'"

Finally, the devil took Jesus up on a very high mountain and showed him all the kingdoms on earth and their power. The devil said to him, "I will give all this to you, if you will bow down and worship me."

Jesus answered, "Go away Satan! The Scriptures say:

'Worship the Lord your God and serve only him.'"

Then the devil left Jesus, and angels came to help him.

Holy City

This is Jerusalem, the capital city of Judea, where the Temple was built. Today it is the capital of modern Israel.

Scriptures Say

This phrase refers to certain of the sacred Jewish Scriptures (what Christians call the Old Testament). It is used when someone wants to show that what they are saying is God's truth.

Satan

The Hebrew word for Satan originally meant "someone who accuses" (opposes). In the Gospels, it is associated with the Devil, the evil one, the one who is opposed to Jesus.

Making Decisions

Temptations

We all occasionally hesitate about which path to take if we want to live as human beings and children of God! There are so many possibilities! If you want to be happy, isn't it easier just to think of yourself? To get out of a difficult situation, isn't it easier to tell a lie? Isn't it important always to try to save your reputation? Temptation tries to make us take paths that lead us away from being children of God.

Choices

Temptation is normal. It's not a sin. There are many situations when people have to choose between truth and falsehood, between selfishness and love of others, between obeying God's commandments or ignoring them, and between good and evil. We all face daily choices! Everyone is free. You must make a personal decision.

The Desert

It's not always easy to choose and make a final decision. How can we be sure we're not making a mistake? How do we avoid taking the easy way out? So before we make our choice, we sometimes need to "go into the desert" for meditation and quiet reflection. A desert can be any uncrowded, quiet, open space. "Going into the desert" means quietly thinking about things by ourselves or with others. It's important to pray that God will help us to find the direction we ought to take.

Help in Choosing

The Bible and the Gospel of Jesus are like lights. They light up each person's conscience. They help us avoid getting lost on dark road. They invite us to choose the light, so that we can stay faithful to God's commandments.

Strength To Resist

It's hard not to take the easy way out. The same Spirit who gave Jesus the strength to resist temptation and stay faithful to his mission is given to each of us. The Spirit lights up the road we must follow and gives us the courage to love, like true children of God.

By Choice

You know them by their choices.

They choose to open their hearts
to God's call,
To live in freedom and walk in truth
in the light of God's law, faithful in love.

They choose to forgive, to put others first,
Not to claim the best seats or push
to the front,
because happiness is everyone's right.

They choose to be "givers"
not "takers" in life;
To serve before they demand to be served;
To share what they could store up for
themselves.

They choose the way of Jesus, who gave
himself for the good of all the world.

You know them by their choices.

They choose to give
rather than take.
They choose to serve
rather than to be served.
They choose to share
rather than hoard things
just for their own pleasure.

They are the ones who choose
to follow the path
of Jesus Christ
who gave himself
so that the world could
be happy!

CHAPTER 3

The Prayer of Jesus

The artist shows Jesus with his eyes closed. He is silent and still. It reminds us that prayer is sometimes about being still and quiet so that we can listen and speak to God in our hearts.

Odilon Redon
(1840-1916),
"Christ with His Eyes Closed"
Pastel

© Photo R.M.N. - Jean, Orsay Museum, Paris (France)

14

Jesus Prays

Synagogue at Ba'ram

Like every other child of his time, Jesus learned to pray at a very early age. He knew the Jewish prayers and that they were addressed to the Lord God. He sang the psalms.* When he grew up and went about his work in Judea, he would make time to go up a mountain or into the desert to speak, in private, with his Father.

His apostles saw him praying. He taught them how to speak to God. What is needed is not repeating phrases that ask God to do what we want. What is needed is finding out what God wants from us. That is what is meant by doing God's will.

Jesus also taught his apostles some set prayers. He chose them from the many Jewish prayers that he knew and gave them a deeper meaning.

Man Praying in Jerusalem

The First Christians at Prayer

The first Christians often gathered to pray. They made up new prayers. They addressed Jesus as "Lord." But they also kept on using the traditional Jewish prayers as well.

At first, they continued going to the synagogue** or to the Temple.*** But, little by little, they got into the habit of meeting in one another's homes. They did this to share their memories of Jesus. Sometimes they wondered what words they should use to address God. They wanted to pray "like Jesus." So the leaders taught them the prayer of Jesus, the "Our Father."

* Psalms
The Bible contains a collection of 150 prayer-songs or psalms. They are still prayed today by Christians and Jews.

** Synagogue
The synagogue was, and still is today, the meeting place or house of prayer for the Jewish people. They meet there to pray and study the Bible, especially on the Sabbath (Friday-Saturday).

*** Temple
This was the great holy place or sanctuary of the Jewish people. It was built in Jerusalem during the days of King Solomon, ten centuries before Jesus, and destroyed by the Romans in A.D. 70.

15

B i b l e

When You Pray...

Matthew 6.5-13

When you pray, don't be like those show-offs who love to stand up and pray in the meeting places and on the street corners. They do this just to look good. I can assure you that they already have their reward.

When you pray, go into a room alone and close the door. Pray to your Father in private. He knows what is done in private, and he will reward you.

When you pray, don't talk on and on as people do who don't know God. They think God likes to hear long prayers. Don't be like them. Your Father knows what you need before you ask.

You should pray like this:

Our Father in heaven,
   help us to honor your name.
Come and set up your kingdom,
so that everyone on earth will obey you,
   as you are obeyed in heaven.
Give us our food for today.
Forgive us for doing wrong,
   as we forgive others.
Keep us from being tempted
   and protect us from evil.

If you forgive others for the wrongs they do to you, your Father in heaven will forgive you. But if you don't forgive others, your Father will not forgive your sins.

People Who Don't Know God

Those who didn't know or believe in God were called pagans. This was the name for those who were neither Christians nor Jews. They usually worshiped statues of other gods (idols).

Father

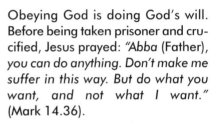

Jesus spoke to God like to his Father. He sometimes called him "Abba," which is like our words "Daddy" or "Dad." Christians too call God "Our Father."

Obey You

Obeying God is doing God's will. Before being taken prisoner and crucified, Jesus prayed: "Abba (Father), you can do anything. Don't make me suffer in this way. But do what you want, and not what I want." (Mark 14.36).

Daily Prayer

Praying

Prayer is the link of love that joins us to God. In fact, if you love someone deeply, you always think about that person. You wish to talk to them and feel close to them. You want to tell them about what makes you happy, and you tell them about the problems that make your life hard. You trust that they will always be there for you. Just so, when we love God, we do the same.

Spare Wheel

Some people only pray when things go wrong in their lives. So they ask God to hurry up and get them out of a difficulty or tight spot. The rest of the time those same people forget about God and never even think about God. They keep God handy, like a spare wheel that they can turn to when they need it! They use God when it suits them. They don't talk to God to share their lives with him as friends do.

Singing and Shouting

When sadness fills your heart, when grief or sickness strikes, or when you fail at something and you feel hopeless, you cry out to God in prayer, and God listens. When your heart is full of joy, when you're about to succeed, or when your hope is reborn, prayer bursts out as praise, and God listens.

Trust

God is love. We can trust God totally and without holding back. God is like the father who looks after each one of his children. No prayer is left unheard, whether it comes from a saint or a sinner! What God hears is one of his beloved children calling out to him.

Sincere Heart

There are some ready-made prayers that express trust in God. They allow us to pray when we gather together, using the same words. But deep in your heart, you can pray in your own words. The most important thing is for

Thanks to Jesus

No one has seen God,
But…

Thanks to Jesus we can know
that God thinks of us
all as beloved children.
And we are to think of God,
full of kindness,
welcoming all with open arms:
the good and the sinners,
the worthy and the unworthy.
God prepares for each one
a place in his celebrations.

Thanks to Jesus we can know
that God is not a Mighty Master
before whom all must bow in fear.
Quite the opposite!
God made himself humble,
small and poor,
so he could be close to the poor
and humble of the world.

Thanks to Jesus we can know
that God demands no sacrifice,
but love.

Thanks to Jesus we can know
that God's work is our happiness.
God's delight is to see
us laughing and dancing,
confident and free!

CHAPTER • 4

Who Is Jesus?

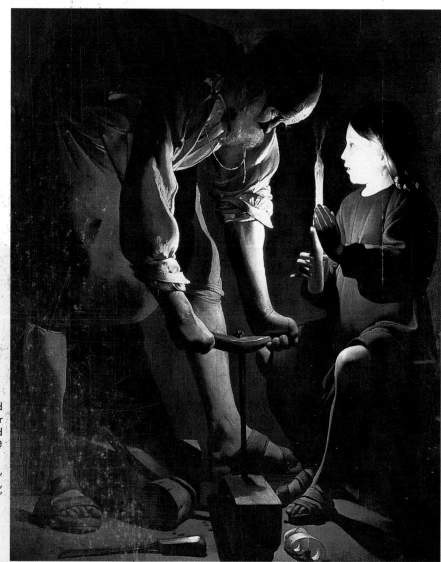

Notice how the artist has used light and shadows. What other contrasts can you find in the painting?

Georges de La Tour,
(1593-1652),
"Saint Joseph the Carpenter"

© Photo R.M.N. - Hervé Lewandowski, Louvre, Paris (France)

So Who Is He?

Cure of a blind man and a paralyzed man. Byzantine mosaic (twelfth century). Monreale Cathedral, Sicily (Italy).

Many people followed Jesus throughout Judea. They knew that he came from Nazareth. They recognized him as the son of Mary and Joseph, the carpenter. He was one of the "locals." Yet they still didn't really grasp who he really was. Jesus' teaching was new. He cured sick people. He was at home with everyone. He said what he thought, even about religion. They knew that John the Baptist had been killed by Herod. Perhaps Jesus was John the Baptist come back to life? In the past God had sent prophets like Elijah, Isaiah, Jeremiah, and Ezekiel. Maybe Jesus was one of these come back again? People were also waiting for a Messiah, a new king, like David.* He was supposed to free his people. Could Jesus be the Messiah they were waiting for? Jesus said nothing. He knew no one was ready to accept a Messiah who had to suffer and be crucified. He wanted people to discover who he was gradually.

Slowly They Understood

After Jesus' death and the news of his resurrection spread, the question of who he was slowly began to become clear. Christians recognized Jesus as the "Messiah" or the "Christ" who was to re-establish the Kingdom of David. For many people, the death of Jesus on the cross remained a scandal. How could the Messiah be crucified by Roman soldiers? It was totally unthinkable! Even the apostle Peter did not understand at first. Jesus had to scold him for suggesting that Jesus should try to avoid the cross. Mark wanted to show that it took time for people to understand it all. He wrote for Christians in Rome who themselves had just suffered a terrible persecution.** They understood Jesus' words in Mark's Gospel very well: *"If any of you one want to be my followers… you must take up your cross."*

H i s t o r y

Jesus said. "I am the Way."

* David
King David lived a thousand years before Jesus. He was considered the greatest king Israel ever had. People never forgot him. In hard times people hoped that a new David would appear.

** Persecution
In A.D. 64, the Roman ruler Nero conducted a persecution of the Christians in Rome. Wrongly accused of setting fire to Rome, Christians were fed to the animals in circuses or burned as living torches in the emperor's garden.

21

Peter's Faith

Mark 8.27-34

Jesus and his disciples went to the villages near the town of Caesarea Philippi. As they were walking along, he asked them, "What do people say about me?"

The disciples answered, "Some say you are John the Baptist or maybe Elijah. Others say you are one of the prophets."

Then Jesus asked them, "But who do you say I am?"

"You are the Messiah!" Peter replied.

Jesus warned the disciples not to tell anyone about him.

Jesus began telling his disciples what would happen to him. He said, "The nation's leaders, the chief priests, and the teachers of the Law of Moses will make the Son of Man suffer terribly. He will be rejected and killed, but three days later he will rise to life." Then Jesus explained clearly what he meant.

Peter took Jesus aside and told him to stop talking like that. But when Jesus turned and saw the disciples, he corrected Peter. He said to him, "Satan, get away from me! You are thinking like everyone else and not like God."

Jesus then told the crowd and the disciples to come closer and he said:

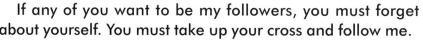

> If any of you want to be my followers, you must forget about yourself. You must take up your cross and follow me.

Elijah

The Bible tells the story of Elijah the prophet going up to heaven without dying. At the time of Jesus, people were expecting Elijah to come back to earth.

Messiah

In Hebrew the word "Messiah" means the "anointed one," that is, someone who has had oil poured on his head as a sign of being chosen by God and filled with the Holy Spirit. The word for "Messiah" in Greek is "Christos," from where we get the name "Christ."

Son of Man

In Mark's Gospel, the phrase "Son of Man" is used to refer to Jesus. When he spoke about himself, Jesus gave himself this name. Other Gospel texts call Jesus "Son of God," "Messiah," "Christ," or "Lord."

The Way of Faith

Questions

We continue to have many questions about Jesus! Is he the Son of God? Is he the Savior of the world? What do his words and actions mean? Is it worth believing in him? Is he stronger than death? Where can he be found? How can we know him? Every believer has these questions. There is a place to find the answers – in the Gospel story!

Liberator

Everything Jesus did had an aim in setting people free from all that keeps them prisoners. He called them to steer clear of the evil that sticks to them and separates them from loving God and neighbor. He comforted those who were suffering in body or spirit. He rescued them from hatred. He offered them the chance of a new life, far from their wretched past.

Conqueror of Death

People fear death. For some men and women, death seems like a great dark hole and the end of everything. In the face of death their hope totters. What's the point of living if we just disappear afterwards? Jesus underwent human death. Yet, he crossed over from death and rose back to life. Death couldn't stop him. With Jesus, death becomes a passage to unending life.

God among Us

Jesus shared our human life completely. He experienced what makes us joyful and what worries us. He took on our troubles and concerns. He went through our tears and sorrows. He enjoyed laughing, and he knew what it was to be hungry and thirsty. With Jesus, God came to be with us and live on earth.

Believing

A lot of people think that believing in God means being sure of everything and doubting nothing! How wrong they are! Believing is a strong desire to know God better and to love God more and more. A person who believes is a seeker! He or she wants to meet and recognize God, not just in prayer and in the Bible, but also in the events of daily life.

Who?

He's here in a way
that you can understand.
It's up to you to see,
up to you to believe!

His name is Jesus.
He was born in Bethlehem and laid
in a manger,
grew up like any other child
and learned to read the ancient stories
of his people and their Covenant
with God.
He traveled around his country –
the deserts, the valleys and hills,
the towns and villages –
and announced the good news
about God who loves everyone.

He called God "Daddy"!
He is God's Beloved Son!

He cured the sick
and gave back dignity
to people who had been pushed aside.
He forgave sins,
something only God could do,
and set people free
from all that oppressed them
in body, mind and spirit.

He was tortured, put to death,
placed in the tomb.
He went through death,
shattering its power.
He is alive!
He is at God's side
and his Spirit of freedom is given
to those who believe in him.

His name is Jesus Christ,
the Savior!
It's up to you to see,
up to you to believe!

The Transfiguration

Here are some clues to use to identify the figures in the picture. Peter, James, and John are struck down with wonder. Jesus has the place of honor. Elijah and Moses are with Jesus. Elijah was a prophet and Moses was the man to whom God gave the law.

Ovanes, Armenian miniature "Gospels: Transfiguration" (Mss 404 fol 3 r) twelfth century

A Moment of Light

Sunset in Argentina

In everyone's life there are moments of light. They sometimes don't last long enough. When they do happen, we understand important questions better: *Why do I exist? What is the universe? Does God exist? Am I loved by God? What have I been called to do?*

Peter, James, and John were the apostles closest to Jesus. One day, they shared an important experience. Jesus took them with him up a high mountain.* They knew the stories of men who had met God on a mountain – Moses and Elijah.**

By being with Jesus, Peter, James and John had already understood that God was not far away. Now, for a moment, they caught a glimpse of who Jesus really was. It was like a great light for them. Jesus seemed to change, to be transformed, to be transfigured. The apostles wanted the moment to last forever, but they had to come down from the mountain and return to everyday life.

Mount Tabor

God's Beloved Son

Mark tells the story of the Transfiguration, but he was not on the mountain. It was probably his friend Peter who talked to him about it. When Mark put his Gospel together, he knew that Jesus had been crucified, and he believed in the resurrection. Like other Christians, he believed that Jesus was not only the Messiah everyone was waiting for, but he was also God's own dear Son. That's something that's not easy to discover and to accept, let alone understand. For that to happen, God's help is needed. So Mark shows that it was God who made us understand who Jesus is. The voice of God that spoke at Jesus' baptism is heard again: *"This is my Son, and I love him. Listen to what he says!"*

* A high mountain
The exact location of this mountain is not known, but it may have been Mount Tabor, which towers over the great plain of Esdraleon. Tabor is 1,850 feet high.

** Moses and Elijah
The Bible records that Moses and Elijah met God on Mount Sinai (or Horeb). Moses met God in the fire, the light, the cloud, and the storm. Elijah met God in the silence of a gentle breeze.

On the Mountain

Mark 9.2-10

Six days later Jesus took Peter, James, and John with him. They went up on a high mountain, where they could be alone. There in front of the disciples, Jesus was completely changed. And his clothes became much whiter than any bleach on earth could make them. Then Moses and Elijah were there talking with Jesus.

Peter said to Jesus, "Teacher, it is good for us to be here! Let us make three shelters, one for you, one for Moses, and one for Elijah." But Peter and the others were terribly frightened, and he did not know what he was talking about.

The shadow of a cloud passed over and covered them. From the cloud a voice said, "This is my Son, and I love him. Listen to what he says!" At once the disciples looked around, but they saw only Jesus.

As Jesus and his disciples were coming down the mountain, he told them not to say a word about what they had seen, until the Son of Man had been raised from death. So they kept it to themselves. But they wondered what he meant by the words "raised from death."

Cloud

In the Bible the image of a cloud is often used to suggest the awesome and mysterious presence of God. In fact, a cloud can both show and hide someone at the same time.

Not To Say a Word

Before Jesus' death and resurrection, there was the chance that people would not understand correctly what exactly happened on the mountain. The Gospel account of this event was written after Jesus had risen back to life (the resurrection).

Raised

People thought of death as the end. No one had come back from the grave. Jesus' resurrection changed everything for the apostles.

Meeting God

Fog

It's not always easy to find the right direction: *Is this the right decision to make? Is it a good choice? What if I'm wrong? Can I really trust my friends? Should I get involved and support this? Is true love possible?* It's like groping around in the fog.

Light

There are some moments of light in day-to-day life that come along and for a second make the fog of hesitation disappear. It may be a celebration, a time of great sharing, or a moment of silence and prayer. At these times, we grasp the fact that we are right in believing in and loving God, and that God's presence is the greatest gift.

A Different Way

Because we keep taking the same roads, because we live with the same people, because we keep praying in the same old way, we may seem to get stuck in our ways! Nothing surprises us any more, either in ourselves or in others. It takes something new, like meeting someone, a special party, or a discussion to open our minds and hearts. We then get to know people in a new and completely different way.

Beginning Again

These moments of light don't last long. But they set a light in our spirits and our hearts that keeps shining! They let us face the daily fog because now, *I believe that God will not abandon me. I know who my friends are. I know that I am able to love.*

Faces

At certain times, a person's face and entire being are changed or transfigured. It's as if joy shines through – the joy that dances inside them, the goodness that's ready to welcome others with generosity, one's trust in God, the warmth of friendship, the happiness which comes from being loved. Faces can make the secrets of the heart appear.

Visible

In Jesus
God's word is spoken.
In Jesus, God draws near.
Today you will see where God is
you'll find God everywhere.

God is visible today
through men and women
who follow Jesus
and transform the world.

God is visible today
where justice brings peace
and creates harmony among people,
the equal and beloved children of God.

God is visible today
through men and women
who pray "Our Father" as Jesus did
and trust God whole-heartedly.

God is visible today
through men and women
who like Jesus
give of themselves to set others free
from that poverty and evil
that disfigures body and mind.

God will be visible today
where men and women
are at work with Jesus
to transform the world
and bring beauty to birth
on our earth.

The Main Events of Jesus' Life

Birth

Jesus was born in Bethlehem about two thousand years ago. His mother was called Mary. Her husband was Joseph, a carpenter.

Nazareth

Jesus was brought up in Nazareth and spent the greatest part of his adult life there with Mary and Joseph. He learned to speak Aramaic, the language of that region. He was brought up in the religion of his people, the Jewish religion. He took part in village life. He had friends among the men and women of the village. They grew up together. When he was twelve years old, he went with his parents on a pilgrimage to the Temple at Jerusalem.

He learned how to work with his hands. He worked as a carpenter for the village and surrounding places. He grew in maturity, learning to love God and his neighbors.

Nazareth

Moving on

Jesus could have stayed in Nazareth and led an uneventful life there. Luke's Gospel tells us that in the fifteenth year of Tiberius Caesar (A.D. 27) Jesus left his home in the village. He began his public ministry. He had a mission to complete and knew that he would not be working alone. After his baptism and a period of reflection, he formed a team that was made up of the twelve disciples and other men and women who worked alongside him. These were ordinary, down-to-earth people. Together they traveled around the country.

In Galilee

The first stage in Jesus' mission takes place in Galilee, his native land. He was well known there and had friends. Not everyone understood what he was doing, although his message was simple. He proclaimed the Kingdom of God (or Kingdom of Heaven). The people in those days knew this meant great changes: getting rid of misery, of poverty, of hunger, and even of the occupying Roman army. Jesus proclaimed a time when justice and peace would rule. His words were received as good news from God. But Jesus did more than talk. He cared for children, sick people, and the poor. He brought them relief and gave them back their hope.

Toward Jerusalem

The religious leaders and the high priests of Jerusalem were suspicious of Jesus and his message about freedom and new life. They criticized him for going around with all kinds of people, for speaking freely, and for saying new things about God. People be-

gan to wonder who he really was. As far as the authorities were concerned, he was dangerous.

Jesus could have stayed among friends in Galilee, but he knew that he had to go on to Jerusalem, the capital. It was a dangerous deci-sion. He knew he would clash with people who opposed him. The disciples were afraid, but they went with their Master. Jesus went into the Holy City, cheered on by the crowd. So that no one could be mistaken, he rode on a donkey, a poor

Jerusalem

person's animal, and not on a horse, as kings and warriors would.

The Last Week

The last week in Jerusalem was difficult. Jesus went to the Temple. He chased the traders and sellers out of the Temple. He spoke with so much authority that the religious leaders plotted against him. He met his friends for the last time and shared the Passover meal with them. Then he was arrested, abandoned by most of his friends, tortured, and nailed to a cross like an everyday criminal. After his death his body was placed in a tomb. His followers were devastated.

Jerusalem, Mount of Olives

Three Days Later

When Mary and Martha visited the tomb three days later, they found it empty! What had happened? Some men and women who were friends of Jesus, said they have seen him alive. They announced, "He is risen." Life is stronger than death. His friends continued his work with the help of the Holy Spirit. They proclaimed the good news. It spread around the whole world like fire. It has reached even to us!

Titles already published:

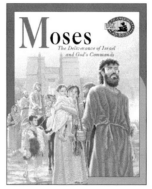

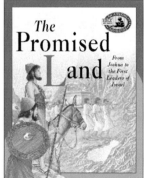

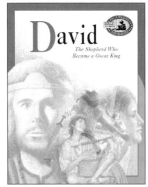

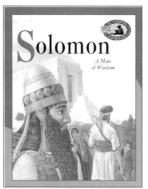

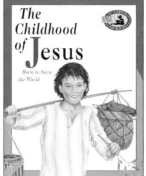

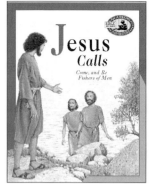

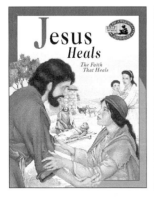

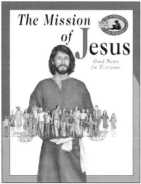

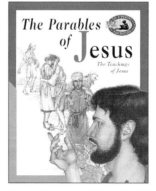

Forthcoming titles in the JUNIOR BIBLE Collection:

- The First Prophets
- Passion and Resurrection
- Exile and Return
- Isaiah, Micah, Jeremiah
- Jesus and the Outcasts
- Jesus in Jerusalem
- Acts
- Wisdom
- Psalms
- Women
- Revelation
- Letters

The Country of Jesus

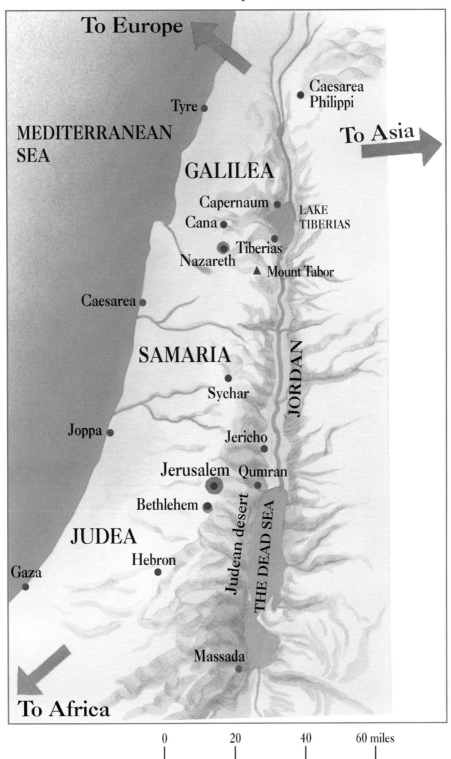

To Europe

Caesarea
Philippi

Tyre

MEDITERRANEAN
SEA

To Asia

GALILEA

Capernaum

LAKE
TIBERIAS

Cana

Tiberias

Nazareth

▲ Mount Tabor

Caesarea

SAMARIA

Sychar

JORDAN

Joppa

Jericho

Jerusalem   Qumran

Bethlehem

Judean desert

THE DEAD SEA

JUDEA

Hebron

Gaza

To Africa

Massada

0   20   40   60 miles

Who Is Jesus?

Vol. 10

This is a Portion of Holy Scripture in the *Contemporary English Version*. The American Bible Society is a not-for-profit organization which publishes the Scriptures without doctrinal note or comment. Since 1816, its single mission has been to make the Word of God easily available to people everywhere at the lowest possible cost and in the languages they understand best. Working toward this goal, the ABS is a member of the United Bible Societies, a worldwide effort that extends to more than 180 countries and territories. You are urged to read the Bible and to share it with others. For a catalog of other Scripture publications, call us toll-free at 1-800-32 BIBLE, or write to the American Bible Society, 1865 Broadway, New York, NY 10023. Visit our website: **www.americanbible.org**

© 1997 ÉDITIONS DU SIGNE

Original text by:	Liam KELLY, Anne WHITE, Albert HARI, Charles SINGER
English text adapted by:	The American Bible Society
Photography:	Frantisek ZVARDON, Gabriel LOISON, Patrice THÉBAULT
Illustrators:	Mariano VALSESIA, Betti FERRERO MIA. Milan Illustrations Agency
Layout:	Bayle Graphic Studio

ISBN 1-58516-138-1
Printed in Italy - Stige, Torino
Eng. Port. CEV 560 P - 109855
ABS 8-9/00